HOW TO PRAY

1.
2.
3.
4.
5.
6.

Lord, teach us to pray, Jesus's disciples asked. This simple prayer, which Jesus taught his disciples, can also show us how to talk with God in prayer.

Our Father in heaven, hallowed be your name. Your kingdom come, your will be done, on earth as it is in heaven. Give us this day our daily bread, and forgive us our debts, as we also have forgiven our debtors. And lead us not into temptation, but deliver us from evil.

MATT. 6:9–13

"YOUR KINGDOM COME, YOUR WILL BE DONE, ON EARTH AS IT IS IN HEAVEN"

As God's children, we long for his righteous reign throughout the earth. But <u>HIS REIGN</u> must first begin in our own lives. We are made sensitive to his will for us as we prayerfully read and meditate on the Word of God. Even as we pray, God exposes our spiritual condition and brings our desires into conformity with his will (Romans 12:2).

"LEAD US NOT INTO TEMPTATION, BUT DELIVER US FROM EVIL"

The Lord has promised to <u>PROTECT</u> his children in the hour of temptation: "No temptation has overtaken you that is not common to man. God is faithful, and he will not let you be tempted beyond your ability, but with the temptation he will also provide the way of escape, that you may be able to endure it" (1 Corinthians 10:13).

The "Lord's Prayer" is how Jesus taught his disciples to pray. And by his example, he showed them the need for time alone with the Father in prayer. We too must set aside time to talk with God and read his Word. The following are suggestions for your time with God:

1. **NECESSITY OF PRAYER.** Jesus taught that prayer is not an option—something to do when we "feel like it"—it is a God-given responsibility. Few of us "find time" to pray, but we must make the time (Ephesians 5:16).

2. **THE BIBLE.** The Bible and prayer go hand in hand. Pray as you read, and meditate on God's Word as you pray. As you read the Bible, praise God for what he reveals of himself and pray for strength and wisdom to obey his commands. Try using the prayers of the Bible as patterns: Matthew 6:9–13; Ephesians 1:15–23; Ephesians 3:14–21; and the Psalms are excellent inspirations.

3. **PRAYER LIST.** A list of prayer requests reminds you of specific needs and will keep your mind from wandering. By recording how God has answered a request, you will be encouraged to keep praying. But don't let this steal your spontaneity. You are praying to a Person, not compiling a list!

4. **PRAYER PARTNER.** To help you pray consistently, ask God for a friend with whom you can share and pray. Meeting regularly provides mutual encouragement.

5. **DISTRACTIONS.** Because prayer is spiritual warfare, Satan will try to distract you. Ask God to help you pray regularly and he will direct you. If you have trouble with wandering thoughts, try changing positions, praying aloud, consulting a prayer list and your Bible, singing a hymn, or whatever you find most effective. But whatever you do, pray!

Bible references: ESV.

CROSSWAY | GOOD NEWS Tracts

www.goodnewstracts.org

ISBN 978-1-6821-6382-5